Good Morning
Bone Crusher!

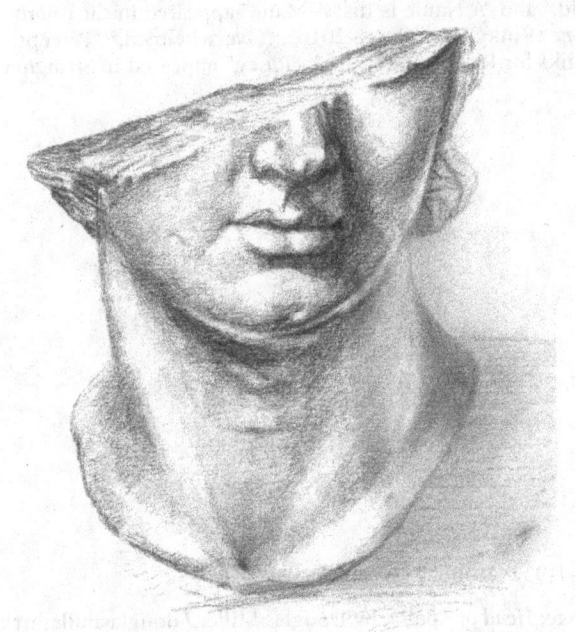

Thomas Walton

Spuyten Duyvil
New York City

Acknowledgements

"A Sentence on Some Movements of Flower Petals" appeared in *Pontoon*. "Sledge" appeared in *Timberline Review*. "Moon Envy," "Still Pond, Rings," "The Crowd Went Wild," and "A Name Is Just A Mane" appeared in the micro-chapbook *A Name Is Just A Mane* (Rinky Dink Press, 2016). "Overwhelmed," "Percept," "Shedding Light," and "Thanks for Raking the Leaves, Honey," appeared in *Stringtown*.

© 2021 Thomas Walton

ISBN 978-1-952419-68-3

Cover image: *Head of Apollo*, by Douglas Miller / douglasmillerart.com

Library of Congress Control Number: 2021941679

"The present is never our end. The past and the present are our means, the future alone our end. Thus we never actually live, but hope to live, and since we are always planning how to be happy, it is inevitable that we should never be so."
                                        PASCAL

"Dazzling and tremendous how quick the sunrise would kill me."
                                        WHITMAN

Contents

Poem With Hands 9
Moon Envy 10
Some Chimes 11
I See You're Scribbling Again 12
One Pill Makes You 13
What Happens When You Die 15
Time Flies 16
The Root of It 17
Did We Drive Up Into the Hills, Or Did We Just See the Hills 18
R.I.P. 19
How Much for the Milkweed? 20
Letter of Intent 21
Reading Roethke Where He Died 22
Time Flies 23
Etymology 24
Time Flies 25
Nikki and Rachel's Couch 26
Poem for Astronauts 28
Melodeon 29
Mule 30
How Can I Get to Heaven from Here? 31
To Wet the Eyes 32
What Might Save the World 33
Before the Bells 34
Reading Ammons Reading Williams 35
Good Morning, Bone Crusher! 36
Anthology 37
I Want You To Know That I Mean It All 38
I Won't Forget It 40
A Sentence on Some Movements of Flower Petals 41
Pater Noster; or A Magic Formula 42
The Arborists 43
Metamorphosis 44
Columnated Ruins Domino 45

You're On Your Own   46
Time Flies   47
Still Pond, Rings   48
Summer Then Was Awful Bright   49
Some Piles   50
Behind the Empire   51
Three Songs   52
In Regards   53
Looking At You Looking At You   54
Sonnet at the Oracle   55
How Can I Say the Lovely Rodents Blinding Me   56
Some Boring   57
That Which Is Always Being Written Remains Unwritten   58
There's a Tree Where the Sun Goes at Night   59
Sledge   60
Dinner Party   61
Still   62
Starting Gate   63
An Ornithologist, A Pederast, Some Locusts   64
Daydream Believer   65
Ancestry of the Rush   66
The Crowd Went Wild   67
Time Flies   68
Thanks for Raking the Leaves, Honey   69
Shedding Light   70
Swimming Hole   71
I Want To Eat A Marsh   72
Snoqualmie Falls   73
Escaping Escaping   74
Happy Birthday   75
Overwhelmed   76
The Crowd Went Wild   77
Percept   78
A Name Is Just A Mane   79

Poem With Hands
after Rilke, after sculptor

you cannot know the calloused hands
that worked this simple stone, bespoke
a living form metamorphic
whisper in the hammer's chatter

chisel, muscle, how the
hewn lines dazzle and seduce
the curved hip perfect
and perfectly flawed

without such listened hands
we have merely stone, language
some rubble unable

                        to sing, to tempt
our eyes to wander, water

unsettle us, and demand by beauty
more beauty from our lives

Moon Envy

stumbling home
drunk
I stopped
to lay in some
stranger's driveway
looking up
at the
stranger's moon

I'd like to
have a moon like that
someday

SOME CHIMES

the wind will
speak out
and the brook
the birds and
thunder
a mini-cooper
some glass
all of these will
speak out and
cry, sing and
ring-around-the
rosie, a Rolls too
and a breeze
the sea the waves
a lake lapping or
borscht, borscht even
will proclaim
a saw, hammer
plank and fowl
all of these
speak out and have
spoken, and do
speak, but
sometimes you
cannot, how
is it that
sometimes you
cannot
even when your
silence does

I See You're Scribbling Again

we sat beside
the galloping stream
unwrapping our skin
then
wrapping our skin
around willow roots
the cottonwood
cantilevered
out
over the creek
and one or two
kingfishers diving
down
to splash and
gather new-hatched
sturgeon
from the flowing places
inside of us

One Pill Makes You

I was in the record store
staring at the cover of
Surrealistic Pillow
noticing the peculiar
shade of pink, but mostly the font
annoyed they chose
"Surrealistic" and not
"Surrealist," wishing I
had been there to say
"how about Surrealist Lightpost or
Surrealist Gloom
or perhaps more artfully
Ceci N'est Pas une Pipe"
I was convinced
I could improve
at very least
what I perceived as
too properly adjectival, as well the
saccharine, too soft pillow.
I was convinced of this when I noticed
I was coming back around
in the record store
despite myself
to an appreciation of
the world as is, as Cage
proposed, and Blake
(in so many words)
the world perfect but for
the way in which we see it.
"Surrealistic" now
was just fine, was in fact
the perfect word, le mot juste

and pillow too, just right and (actually)
couldn't be better.
There were two copies
of what surely was and is
the best named album of all time,
the Sonnets to Orpheus of
classic rock, and the
Flowers of Evil of psychedelia
I bought both copies
why not?
one to remind me of my
poor judgement
and one to eat for dinner that night.

What Happens When You Die

I sat listening
on the rocky crags
moss-heavy
to a speedboat
hidden in the fog
buzzing closer
louder
then passing
   (the speedboat)
out into
the fog
diminishing
slow until
a seagull finally
laughed it up

Time Flies

I remember
   seeing you
      in the field
picking flowers
   near the pond
      where sand cranes
graze along
   flat mud banks
      I was a dumb bicyclist
   gliding by
      in the heat
those long
   country lanes
      elbowing
through the fields
   I remember
      seeing you
approaching you

I'd like to linger
   in that approaching
      never pass, never
concede to time
   its threshing
      let's not mar
that perfect dream
   but continue staying
      boundless singing
there she is again
   there she is again
      there she is again
still

The Root of It

At your grave it occurred to me that all the lines, in obeisance to some manufactured linear god, had been imposed by non-linear phenomena—the wind or wave or wastrels, the wasps unaware or in us, etc.—and in this way a kind of neurosis has settled like dew, like dreams or detergent onto the wild slope and raveling fields, eradicating the tearing up, the filling with blood, the alchemy of sunset, of leaves, drifts of irises etc. and that one drop of wonder is aspiration enough and may even raise the dead.

Did We Drive Up Into the Hills, Or Did We Just See the Hills

on the bank, the bent beer can
lodged in willow roots
full of its own discard
the hand long gone, its beer gone
its throwing gone, and even now
its drift gone
I saw a horse by the river
a foal drinking
the young offspring of a horse
its eyes were unconcerned, its neck
the four hoofs in the round rocks
that sound as it shifted
was spectacular, a corroboree
some things are impossible to prepare for
the Virgin Mary in a piece of toast
food poisoning, this foal
doing nothing, standing, bending to drink
lifting to look, turning to leave
leaving

R.I.P.

the storm finally
dropped down
and took nearly
all the dogwood
leaves with it

in the street a
stretch of water
rushed away
to the drain
on the corner

where the lights
from the gas station
reflect
on the dark pavement
red and blue and
seventy-six

How Much for the Milkweed?

I remember the milkweed growing
along the driveway at the garage sale
the warm air and crickets
like rings in a still pond
that fat Michigan family
the one in her chair, in her chair all day
all that plastic spilling from the garage
not a single thing worth owning
I remember there were diapers
an open package of diapers
for sale, the diapers
smelling of powder and "scent"
beside the Barbie castle
and the woman, sitting
her body devouring the chair
and the milkweed growing
standing, stuck in the humid air
the shallow ditch, the crickets
cricking, the butterflies
terrorizing their blooms

LETTER OF INTENT

I'd like to think
these little poems
in addition to being
quick sketches of willows
are also, by turns
deeply concerned
with the barn-like
collapse
of a hapless culture
and if not a culture then
at least a single life

Reading Roethke Where He Died

the seascape
lifted
unlapping
and flooded my
lungs and eyes
what a way
to find Roethke
bloated on
gin rickies and
chlorine
floating in a
Bloedel pool
till a garden came
and filled with sand
what once was mere
music and
bone

Time Flies

the end doesn't justify the means
the means *are* the end

heroes dress however they like
I like to think that
rather than intelligent design
we're in a kind of
laughable happenstance

accidents of flora we mistake for god
the grilled cheese grilled in a way
that made it obvious
Our Lady of the Marbled Rye
would soon descend from the
swirling sky

still lake, dark cloud
a single swan glides beneath
the willow to wait
for the storm to pass

just another rowboat
just another tree

all your life for this
every moment
the moment that's meant to be

Etymology

the word 'joviality'
comes from Jupiter
isn't this enough
to prove the existence
of extra-terrestrial life?

Time Flies

He yelled at me in English
though he didn't speak it.
I'm not sure exactly
what he meant by "columnated
ruins domino."
He was offended
I think, by my boots and their
state of disrepair.
I love the way the churches rise
from the plazas in Guadalajara.
The chatter marks
of cathedral stones
telling stories in
the morning sun.
The coffee was rich and strong
we must've stayed there forever.
I like to think that we're still there
though I remember leaving
driving through
the hills outside of town
all caked with dust and dust-colored things
great heron-like swatches of
rows of blue agave in the distance.
Once again, I didn't pay
enough attention
to the men shining shoes in the square
their dry hands black with polish
sometimes working, mostly lazing
on wooden benches beneath the ficus
huddled around radios
listening to the game.

Nikki and Rachel's Couch

the bread dough
rose overnight
a kind of miracle
though we act as if
we know
how it happened
and even
assume some
responsibility

daylight's the same
as if it were
no big thing
that when you went
into the shower
it was still dark
but now, saying
"are you still writing?"
the sky open
the traffic thick
clearly visible

looks like someone
finally took
the couch the neighbors
dragged out
to the hydrant last week

to every object its handler
we can't resist
we who have hands
putting them
all over things
a kind of carpe diem

knowing soon
we'll look down
hands gone, eyes gone
couches drifting
in our dreams

Poem for Astronauts

getting in the spaceship
can be a tricky business
    the ship, first
    seems to be essential
all human beings are descended
from a single pair
of overbearing parents
    the sun, for instance
    and moon
(though the moon is more
like the gorgeous aunt
you never quite see enough of)
    but once you're in
    you're in the ship
    and once in the ship
    gravity ends
floating over fountain grasses
a river versus eddied silence
    "throw my body anywhere lord
    in that old field"
all poetry aspires
not to birdsong, but to belong
to the field outside of body
    (anywhere lord)
an old tub is birdsong
    once when the moon was waning
    the dew-covered scotch broom
    bowed so low the deer lifted
    glistening in the field
standing and grazing
seemingly saying
    there's nothing better
    than doing nothing
    with absolute devotion

Melodeon

why couldn't I have been
a Flemish painter of portraits
living quietly alone
in Flem, or else
a small reed organ
having the excitement
and emotional appeal
of heavy woolen cloth
something like Moby Dick
or merely
Melville's beard
membranous
that is, unforgettable

is it true we only
get one chance at this
and disappear gradually, like
rings in a
still pond, lake
I'd like to be a lake
a summer lake
well dressed with
rowboats and willows
someplace
even ugly folks
can find willing lips
to kiss

Mule

the sterile hybrid
offspring of a male
donkey
and a female horse
having long ears
and a short mane
stood
with matted hair
eating the pile
of discarded baby's breath
outside the flower shop
on Tenth
a frayed rope
around its neck
tied to an oak
the only thing
keeping it
from drifting off
over the bars
where young faces
drunk and dour
stare at their phones
hoping to find
the next great thing
to do

How Can I Get to Heaven from Here?

you saw it again last night
this time outside the double doors
saloon-like, of the bar
in what's best described as
"the shitty part of town"
that part the money hasn't found
trash and graffiti
broken plexiglass
of the bus stops, bottles
empty, shadowy figures
zombie-like, confined to spend
their entire lives
leaning on dead cars
and then too of course
the dead cars
which deserve, at least
a line of their own
nothing makes sense here
the rain, the dark drunken night
warm and full of cheap wine
what is this place? this prayer?
this song of god dropping
like dew or damp leaves
a drink too much
down into you, over you
again walking there, just walking
that horrid street
asking yourself
are you alive enough
to feel the breadth
of beauty all around?
and the answer a resounding
no

To Wet the Eyes

what goes untold can save the world
can be a vesicant for the skin
describe dawn: that blue light
water slipping through our
awkward mitts, a mewl
whimpering out, mouse-like
in the dry desert air
look Janet
I don't mean to be crude, but
we don't have to live like this
look how easy what's easy is
see it now, up now
over the skeletal alder woods
screaming again, ignored again
simple sunrise, sky on fire

What Might Save the World

when I walked out of
Al's Body Shop
a bus passed
close
and disturbed
a puddle in the street
near where
someone had raked
a pile of leaves
up against
the weathered trunk
of a hawthorn tree
by the time
the water
had regained its calm
I was gone
noticing other
unimportant things
along the leafy streets
where Mark and Janine
used to have
their bookshop

Before the Bells

I remember driving through
the valley that morning
the little churches in the fog-light
the near-light, still more
dark than light but also
optimistic, those perfect
silhouettes, their
steeples and white cedar siding
the high doors and steps
leading up between junipers
the junipers
still black, only just waking
the nuns coming out
walking around to the garden
devoted to god and galanthus
care of little churches
happy in the quiet valley
the valley still asleep
dreams still ringing
in the heavy morning
          orchard air

Reading Ammons Reading Williams

I turned off
the highway
and parked
in a lot overlooking the lake

Atlantic cedar
salient over
the dull grey
dead body
the lake seemed to be

every wave
on hiatus, some

construction workers
wearing parkas
were drinking coffee
and smoking joints
nearby, laughing

what a
way to read
Ammons, a dog
leapt out
of the workers' truck
to sniff
(and piss on)
some dandelions
waving in
the thin morning
breeze

Good Morning, Bone Crusher!

when the light
finally broke
through the Salix trees
    (gramma always called them Salix)
the sun poured in
and paid particular favor
    (that's how she would say it)
to the jade plant
in the dimpled
terra cotta pot
    (she, in fact, bought for us)
on the coffee table now
for years
but never such a
teeming city
dwarfing all the
books around it
though they themselves
now glowing, too
like peacocks in this
wild and wondrous
light

Anthology

the study of flowers
can be overwhelming
though consists merely
of staring long hours
noting both
pattern and aberration
pistil and ovary
labia and stamen
it is, in a word
exhausting
rich with fragrance
color and curve
and like love, lust
and loneliness
its sea is always
growing larger

I Want You To Know That I Mean It All

I should apologize
for another poem about lilacs
not lilacs but paddlefish
fish of a family
not them but dying
not dying but life
not life but a gathering
of lilacs, fish, dying
so as to stretch as much
as possible this miscellany
the lilacs and paella
made with rice
not rice but saffron
not that but praise
of paddlefish and dying
an exultation in any order
not order but river
a river of lilacs
not river but rush
not that but the sound
the sound and the word
the phrase "a river rushes jubilant"
not that but lilacs
a hundred lilacs
some thousands
dying, not dying
in ruins
columnating
in dooryards
in bloom
what, after all
is a dooryard

what blooming
what dying
not that but browning
drying, a paean
of fervent gracious hymns
not hymns but rushes
not river but fervor
not this but that
the both the same
and dying
not dying but lilacs
a boat or canoe

I Won't Forget It

that day you walked
across the field
an old metal pail
full of dandelions and
daisies swinging
in your right hand
the grass wet
tall, nearly
up to your waist
I'll miss you when it's over
though it's silly, as it seems
so far from over
I'll miss you though
when it's over
and the geese, too
pushing through the sunlight
between firs along the river
their absurd honk and gaggle
filling up, spilling out
all the valley can hold

A Sentence on Some Movements of Flower Petals

I was wondering about the ozone layer and how no one mentions its depletion anymore

when the sun came out from behind a cloud and I noticed a petal from a cherry blossom from the tree next door (where Diane used to live)

floating past my window

rolling like a paddlewheel and then also, at times, unturning

swinging downward like the pendulum of the grandfather clock my parents had when I was young

(grandfather clocks, evidently, have gone the way of the ozone layer)

paddling and swinging, lifting and not, like confetti in the breeze above the traffic down below but only one single petal so

not like confetti at all but confetto—candy, pink as a hog or the color I imagine pinworms to be—

floating in the clear depleted light out over the street and away toward the dogwood tree arching over, struggling to hold the weight of a

thousand meringue-white blossoms of its own.

Pater Noster; or A Magic Formula

beyond the old shed
a garden snake bathed
on the grassy pile
of warm stones
its patience patent
open to the afternoon
the sun having moved
around the hemlock
growing on the edge
of the steep drop
down to the river
where last year
the two Mexican boys
fishing, wrecked their
boat and
drowned

The Arborists

a pasture is a common gesture
something to walk out into
to cross to figure the flowering tree
alone on the hillock
where the cattle gather
to drink water at the trough
brushing aside the frenzied flies
beneath the petal-like bracts
of the dogwood (*Cornus florida*)
alone on the hillock
sheltering the cattle
harbored under
the cool hem of its shade

Metamorphosis

we took the bat
yellow
up to the park
a whiffle ball

I pitched
you swang (bang!)
the ball flew
screamed up

toward the chestnut tree
into it … gone

seconds later
a little flurry
of flower petals
falling down

Columnated Ruins Domino

I found a new form
of worship
an old form
a written form
a sung form
the body given over
a life for the sun
or book, child
what does it matter
so long as it's given
to say 'promenade'
or 'public park'
to say 'alameda'
this, only this
and walk beneath the
tremoring word
or in it like a
wild cashew

You're On Your Own

I warned you that
if you drank
all your poems would praise
love or god or wine
so you didn't drink
and read me the poem about
large nonvenemous arboreal snakes
pretty good, but
too adjectival
too sentimental, too much
morning light
(why is it always blue?)
I suggest, I guess
that you disregard
my previous advice
and drink heavily
and drink often

Time Flies

I see the spacious summer
a falcon leaving the tower
the water tower, now center
the city park spilling out
around it, high on the hill
the tower, the spacious summer
lasting many years, yet
falling again to order
what's perfect is what lacks
nothing essential to the whole
this entire summer
vast as an aria, a mesa on
the precipice of May
now September, now
looking down, edging forward
jumping off, dropping down
into the damp, dark
gravel pits of fall

Still Pond, Rings

at each stump we stopped
to gather pitch
for a winter's worth
of fires, the moon
lingered over
the dogwood tree
at the far end
of the field
where the cattle go
for water
and where we found
the coyote skull
last year, hair still
ringing
the empty pits
its eyes had become

Summer Then Was Awful Bright

the lake waits, the spring
seeps out of the hillside
finds the lake, the lake
covers over with duckweed
rowboats, the rowboats
wait, moored to
the dock in the shade
willows hang, shade
the rowboats, the ducks
feed near the bank
the grass on the bank
wet from the storm, the spring
runs over the grass, we say
"the grassy stream"
and walk through it
to the dock, untie
the boat, row out
float in the sun, wait
the wait interminable
the kiss, then, the kiss
a lake, the lake
round, ringing

Some Piles

from our boat
we saw the whale
breach
and then slip back
into the sea
the piles
stuck out
along the shore
where a little
white house
sat on the cliff
smoke
trailing up
from a burning pile
of leaves a woman
stood next to
holding a rake
and a glass of what
I like to think
was gin

Behind the Empire

the Romans thought that
bread and circus
was enough
to keep the goons
subdued
nothing much
has really changed
I don't like the circus
but all of us
have to go it seems
so I went
until I couldn't
eat another
clown, then
excused myself
and walked out
around
to the other side
of the tent
where a piebald horse
was standing alone
remarkable only
for its ordinariness
I said, "ordinariness"
but it did nothing
just stood there
eating oats
by the driver's side door
of the old white car
Marge gave us
before you left

Three Songs

down by the lake
where the hollow
stemmed grasses
rush
the reed song
like a whisper
through the marsh
blackbirds trill
perch like
red-winged
dahlias, terminal
flowers down
by the lake where
they found
the pale body
of the child partly
eaten and
echoing with flies

In Regards

I thought I'd drive down
to Leschi and sit
beside the lake, turn
the radio off, turn
all of it off
the storm passing
out over
the dull, feckless
waves, regardless
of Bellevue
small and silly on the
opposite shore
the bridge busy
with light and
the willow
waving where some
brants had
gathered, grazing
on the bank

Looking At You Looking At You

what's happened to our
rancid lips   New York!
how fun it was to be so
regaled in sables and
ruffs of an evening
unapologetically hip
I miss Ted Berrigan
and the flatulence of his
repose   O Brooklyn-Portland,
       Oregon!
these days it seems we've
lost our way, all the fun
thought right out the fun bag
please lord, let me never
see myself again
the way these others
see themselves, hung up
on their selfies
let me merely
  mistake me instead
for some such nothing
some wood bench
half burned beside the trash heap
full of nails, full of knots
full of ants and rot and wonder

Sonnet at the Oracle

crossing over on the ferry
to find the place they said there was
an oracle shining, though covered over
with grass and rasping briars

disembarking from the ferry
we searched and thought we found out back
behind the Philip's 76
the hidden oracle shining

we were ecstatic, and so we asked
"What fate, O Wisdom, O Voyance
have we in store?" but the oracle
was quiet, a Volkswagen beetle

and the sky grew heavy, and dim
and darkness where our bodies had been

How Can I Say the Lovely Rodents Blinding Me

the privet hedge
that's finally stopped
blooming
swells now with
rock wrens
some of which
drop down
and hop along
the mossy lawn
to search the grass
for bugs

Some Boring

I was thinking about the avant-garde, and how so much of it is, in fact, an attack on art itself—The Poem, or Painting—and how these avant-gardists/lawn mowerists ride around cutting down the very thing they do, the thing beneath them, the thing on which they stand and which they also claim to be, which is all fine of course because who really cares about the avant-garde? Sandbags.

Anyway, all of these cul de sacs will one day commit the final act, or be committed by it, whether looking into the hole they've bored into themselves or the one they've bored out into sky or sea, slobbering in their whale skins, plastered lizard-like, loafing along a sunlit wall longing only for listening, just one more day of that.

That Which Is Always Being Written Remains Unwritten

I took some time off
to watch the rosinweed
bending in a breeze
where the path dips down
and then out onto
a floating dock, through
cattails and rowboats
grebes diving down
to eat the marsh
popping up, the flat lake
breaking out
into bird and ringlet
I stopped there awhile
to concentrate on the
overwhelming mash
hoping to forget
trying hard
to leave the world of writers
to writers
to find a kind of
filterless scene
to bury my eyes and
hands here
in the red wing whisper
of the unwritten shore

There's a Tree Where the Sun Goes at Night

when we walked to
the upper field
the sun still
shone through
the fir trees
at the far edge
of the paddock
a slender knife
of light cut
across the herd
sheltered under
a dogwood tree
that glowed orange-
red and gathered
every last
drop of day

Sledge

I looked all day
at the asses
of the dogs pulling me
and all day they ran
all day the sun
glared, the ice
glared, the hills
stayed far off all day
the sled slipping
singing something
soft all day
we were getting nowhere
the asses and I
all day I thought
"soon I will arrive
soon all of this
will be done
soon I'll know
why the hell I
thought to come this way"

Dinner Party

the spring at the farm
shoots out the cliff
    (there are no of's about it)
and spills down
where the vine maples
grow thick in the swamp
we call it the swamp
but it's just
somewhere to go when
the chatter at the house
becomes too much, when
even the skunk cabbage
is a breath of fresh air

STILL

this morning
the rain is
gentle in the
conical streetlamp light

the sky not yet
luminous
the rooms across the street
still dark when

the first garbage trucks
scream past the
plum tree budding
beneath my window

Starting Gate

the doors opened and I
thought I heard a bell when
Janet raced out
into the rich, green
meadow where
last summer
the dog found
the calf half-
eaten, coyotes
hiding in the
scotch broom
waiting for us
to leave

An Ornithologist, A Pederast, Some Locusts

in the park, when the
sun came out
it seemed to be a
thin, crisp cracker
the daisy tufts
mole hills
people reading on
blankets seemed to
shimmer
in the new garrulous light

"this is enough," I thought
but then quickly
"why isn't this enough?"

an ornithologist,
a pederast, some locusts
they were all there
in the park, in the sun
bejeweled by its light
held fast and warm
in the common glory
of its thin gelatin
all of us living
right here, right now

Daydream Believer

let me guess:
you actually think
at some point this
single-masted sailing ship
slobbering along
will find
if not a flowering port
then at least the last
dream of day
catching all its
orange-red slippage
full-sail, and you will
glow along with it
the boat, in some
calm stretch of saltwater
exhaling like a
seal ridding itself of the sea
a last lovely battle hymn
before the battle ends

you believe that?!

Ancestry of the Rush

I walked down
to the shore
where the marsh plants
stood firm
unmoving in the
morning fog
the path wound
its way within
the pliant, pithy
stems arching up
from a mat of
others that had fallen
died
at some point
along the way
piling up
breaking down
a hundred
thousand
stories
tangled there
shooting up like
marsh plants in the
morning fog

The Crowd Went Wild

the horse won
first prize
so stood
steaming
on the dirt track
with a
wreath of
alstroemeria
around its
neck, not
looking
particularly pleased
just
standing there
steaming
and having a
tremendous
piss

Time Flies

I love the way the
joggers run some
weekend mornings
past the rain-soaked
gardens littered
with maple leaves
their orange shoes
tracing through the
grey glum
gathering light
I love to
grab on to them
their orange shoes
as they flash and
spin down the
empty weekend
rain-soaked street
I hate the way they
disappear
around the corner
where Joan seems
to always be
and always be
wearing that
huge red raincoat

Thanks for Raking the Leaves, Honey

this afternoon
the wind shifted
and swelling blew
all the maple leaves
from the yard
down to the dunes
where most tangled in
the gnarled branches of
coastal plants
though some
made it through
to the beach where
someone had
dragged a small boat
up from the bay
and left it there
just above the line of
leaves the waves were now
pushing and
pulling in
curves and arches
across the pockmarked sand

Shedding Light

I was thinking about the avant-garde and how mostly movement forward is both implied and certainly celebrated, whereas regression is less so, in fact not so, even though all illusions of linear progression in an immeasurable universe are surely just that, illusions.

I was thinking about this when I lifted the rock beside the compost bin and what seemed several hundred centipedes dropped and dived and wriggled in a confused flourish of newly illuminated mayhem not a single line of which was anything close to straight, much less fore or aft or philistine.

Swimming Hole

we parked the car
the sound of
gravel lurch quick
ended and we
walked down
not far
to where the river
elbows, a thick
stand of
alders hid
a blue tarp
inside which
the man's body
wrapped and
gnawed at
for days by
coyotes or
some less
visible force
we all will
soon know well
maybe we
shouldn't swim here

I Want To Eat A Marsh

the marsh plants
where we go to
watch the scoters dive
have sheath-like
stipules and
small, dense clusters of
pink, white, and green
blossoms, when a
breeze breathes across them
every flower starts to
laugh and breaks you
into pieces

Snoqualmie Falls

we climbed down
the cliffs, the path
narrow, winding
through the rocks
the ferns and
snowberry wet
with mist
until we reached
the pool the falls
had carved out by
continuous pounding
racing fast to splash
spread, billow or
drive straight
down into
the deep throat of
overmatched stone
which miracle
are we waiting to see
so that we finally see
what miracles there are
that are everywhere
around us?

Escaping Escaping

crossing over on the ferry
out of boredom more than any
desire to see the same
tourist traps you
saw last time you were this bored
last time you felt the need
to indulge misery
in that certain way
that small town way
so you sail to Bainbridge
or any other of these little
logging towns
        turned
taffy towns
        turned
antique towns
        turned
boutique towns
        turned
zombie towns
        turned
to stone
if you're lucky you're alone
if you're lucky there's a bar
and you can have a few
drinks and read awhile
before vowing
again
to never come back

Happy Birthday

when they told me
I was dying
(have they told you yet?)
I suddenly saw
the common housefly
as the most
extravagant
bird in all of
ornithology
a tiny tress
of what's marvelous

Overwhelmed

outside the bar
the snow started
to fall and all the
drinking us
looked out in
wonder as a
loud wave
of dumb joy
spilled through
the sodden booths
stools spinning
drunken smiling
glasses rising
to toast the
little white
falling flakes

The Crowd Went Wild

near the waterfall
the trillium blooming
arching and
waving like
a restless crowd
an audience that
rose and cheered
when the eagle shat
a thick quart
of white paint
splat
on the damp green
moss-covered stone

Percept

this has been nice
living here with you
the gardens full of
dahlias in the park
those long empty days
reading in the sun
they, more and more
seem to me to be
the best employment
dandelions are welcome
in my lawn, why not
what's wrong with weeds
the columnated ruins
domino, of course
I have no lawn
but if I ever do
the weeds will be welcome
morning glory
chrysanthemum
it's been nice
despite it all
this world that falls
like a lover on my chest

A Name Is Just A Mane

now I think
at last I understand:
I'm here
first to learn
the names of things
and then to learn
the names of things
aren't important

Notes

pg. 9 "Poem With Hands" is written after Rilke's famous "Archaic Torso of Apollo"

pg. 22 "Reading Roethke Where He Died" is written after A.R. Ammons' poem "WCW"

pg. 25 I use the phrase "columnated ruins domino" in different places throughout this book. It's taken from Brian Wilson of the Beach Boys in his song "Surf's Up." As the legend goes, Mike Love (also in the band) objected to the abstract nature of the phrase—he wanted to sing simple songs about cars and girls. An argument ensued that essentially broke up the band. I've always been fascinated by this story, as it illustrates not only the ability of language to get under our skin, but also the challenges of Keats's idea of Negative Capability. Mike Love was obviously "irritably reaching after the truth." The phrase resists definition even though the image seems pretty straightforward. Love could not wrap his mind around the metaphor, and it made him hate (hate is not too big a word here) Wilson.

pg. 35 "Reading Ammons Reading Williams" is also written after A.R. Ammons' poem "WCW"

pg. 38 The first two lines of this poem are "stolen" from Canadian poet Stephen Collis. They are from a poem I heard him read at a live performance. A year or so later we were reading at the same event. I told him I was going to read a poem that begins with his lines "I want to apologize for another poem about lilacs." I said "I hope you don't mind that I stole them." He laughed, "no, I don't mind, I stole them from Phyllis Webb."